ROBIN PURVES

Three Spiders Fucking

BROKEN SLEEP BOOKS

Published 2020,
Broken Sleep Books:
Cornwall / Wales

brokensleepbooks.com

First Edition

Lay out your unrest.

Publisher/Editor: Aaron Kent
Editor: Charlie Baylis

Typeset in UK by Aaron Kent

Broken Sleep Books is committed to
a sustainable future for our planet,
and therefore uses print on
demand publication.

brokensleepbooks@gmail.com

ISBN: 978-1-913642-00-6

Contents

Three Spiders Fucking

Robin Purves

On Earth it means an opening in a house, a door, or a place on the forest floor that lets light in. It means daybreak, and the incandescent lantern, burning magnesium in the smoke hole. A luminous glade with a pale, bright flame. White spots in the eye, kindling, interior lux. Perhaps also atonement, and victims brought to light.

Make a perforation in the plaintext for this person, or for this person, or for this person: start from there. Being as close as possible to them, being beside them, will make them feel good when you and those persons stay passionate and so on. A person's morning is happy when a person facing a person, or facing the morning happiness of a person, is happy.

He told himself he
could turn round would look
back he would see her again

Then everything was not
there: no way and
no place and no other earth,
no sun and no sky,

He turned round
sweating a skilful
kiss goodbye and

Like another earth
everything was there again:
the way and the place,
he could see

On the way to a tree
guess what:

Dead love is in the frame then
you hold tight and cheat yourself.

He took his scarf and
folded it against
rocks forest a bridge
and a sweet, long-suffering sky
hung over this blind basin
in pale stripes.

Do not go away. The throat
that you flirt with
in the shadow
of a head or an end
without passion will
be

Dead in the year. You
go on without me, to the

empty socks.

Go to bed.
A man in a blue coat
has eaten the way.

Or just as often the flame goes out
and a man is hanging from a bough in a clearing
his blue coat off and
the trees close as
all the streaming services close.

The dog was agitated when
I reached the clearing I saw
the ruin, a dead man is like
a baby, you hold it
where it's not bleeding

I found you here and
then I looked for you

Faded green T-shirt
from which birds spring

Yellow eyelid the
eyeballs ripened

In the sky the
hot pink ball gag sun

In addition tonight you see
the scaffold hemp scarf

The flowering jade balance
a perfume could upset

Climbing spirits in the flask
the person from the hanging scroll

now gone in weighted
sack to the forest floor

Half-sitting in the neck of the wood
the operation wilts

The grass soaks up you know what
the flow of gold soft water

Has nothing to do
with this planet

At the bend of a path
and a needle-strewn bed
the sun shone on rot,
and the rot from the bed
looked at the sun.

After a long walk in
wet shoes, a dead man
spreads.

Withering tissues of the heart
of the foot come out

of the boot, the ankle moth
bitten fly symmetry

In the pines
a mile and a
half from here
I found you
and then I looked for you,
still in a tree:
throw the T-shirt aside
there slipped off
in the branches
destroy everything,
to the roots

The dragonfly taper touched
wings and made for the exit

A dream of the aftermath of a poetry reading. The participants sit in shadows at one end of an ornate conference room, assembled as if we are not there or as if someone will be coming to let us out. I reluctantly question the poet about the contents of a black sports bag at his feet. Every answer has to be removed from him. He admits that it contains food, then that it is pork, then that he has personally selected the pig from a local farm, taken it home and slaughtered and slaughtered himself and then cooked the different parts in different ways. Then he opens the bag, puts his hand in his hand and hands me a portion of ribcage. I ask him if he wants me to eat it and then to tell him how it tastes. He nods. I think to myself, "It looks like lamb rather than pig." I take a large bite and look back at the flesh and realise that close to the bone it is raw and bleeding. I explain to him that the bones have not had time to conduct the heat through the meat and cook it. I am surprised to see that the surface looks like tangled hair on a wet dog the colour of shit and ginger. I bring him the message that it's not even pig, is it a German shepherd? * My plastic cup contains a ball covered in wet paint. There is a bright, clean and dense smell. Two women are in the pool, fully dressed. The artist sits on a tiny chair at a tiny table with a tiny glass of orange tea. In the tea, a small piece of amber, and, trapped inside it, a smaller piece of amber, and trapped inside the smaller piece of amber, spunk. He eats it. He is wearing a bright yellow balaclava and instantly becomes dazzling. Two men lead him away, and return without him five minutes later. * I have lost my backpack with all my clothes and books somewhere near the station entrance. The left luggage section is also a men's locker room, so the men get dressed around me. I realise that the train will leave in a few seconds, that I will miss it. I call my mother in a panic but my mother can't help me and at the end of the call I notice that the ground is moving under my feet. I am on the last train, I have not missed the train. I start screaming on the phone: *I'm on the train! I am in the train! But I have nothing with me, I have nothing with me!* Then I wake up with a sore jaw and a slit head, feeling like I have been hit with a hammer.

Poppers and grass on the headlands and pastures. In double sight, the plantation with undergrowth cleared, a clearing on the right, unwooded wood that gapes to the sky, stops, approaches, stops. What to look out for and what to avoid: waiting for someone to come; looking at something; having to meet someone, and so on. To enter or go. After a few hours: look, a dog. The path through the clearing towards a board over a ditch and standing water where it runs to catch up, or running in the woods past the swift growth of lenders and crossing fallen logs head down under the ferns and over the scrub, broken contours of fawn and whitenesses through the matted hair.

The you you destroyed
Or the you who destroyed
One of you should say something
With the deed still to do
In view of a beetle, a snail,
Three moths,
Three spiders fucking.
Help me to remember,
Dog of the particles and permeability,
More silent in this poem
Than self-silencing, the
Fact of death still not dead
Enough still not enough like
Being dead and all the wood
Turned into coffins & paper

Here is my third death
Mark not by cutting
Or piercing pale green
Extending down the stem or axis
Below the point of attachment
Scion or sucker offshoot, striking root
Transverse bar from end of which
Nothing depends, weakening
Leaf by leaf, the hot strip or
Ribbon let-out stranger fruited
Thorn and buried metalwork: the
Slip by which current leaves
Pitted by a shower
Of morbid hail
The helplessness of a dog
Speaking of the event
As from a mouth
Obscured by sewage
Above the exit point of water
In a thin stream or spray
No clear statement is possible

Water that did not exist before
Vapour and ice on other planets' moons
Clouds of tears and
Splash of brightening gas above
The solar limit near the point of origin
A thin film or slick of oil
Soothing bitter remark
Deliverance from anxiety and
Sweet mutual non-relation
Tears precipitately violable
Bruised or coarsely ground
Crushed into small pieces
Serrated, incised and expressed in
Fourteen para-segments

I can't pronounce it
I can't say it
I can't speak of it
Mark in the dust
Braced against the fall
Heard the green echoing
Communist children
Unchained from the plausible
Chair gets up, flips
A coin or table, bank
On the grammar borne
On the desquamating wind
The money is spent and
Unrecoupable light upon a
Forearm quick with tendons
Snapped along the mainline
Another great evil scored blood
Vessels driven from their beds into
The sights, by a knot placed at the side
An effort to swallow inclined
At edge to prevent falling,
Fixed in position and not for sale
Abrasions, happy bark
Secured to the sleeper,
Stakes, pegs, hooks, a slip

Of the throat, plants breaking,
Declining to assert a claim
Taking your leaves in
A small window, small shade

Depression on earth's surface
Is bounded by faults I declare,
Moving around the hospital
Heated by fermenting manure,
Spreading infection in the children's sward
By short term action,
My heart is sore like
The headlong flight of the dog,
Aimless and impaired
By the damp brake nowhere
Except in the rest
Of the universe and
Your own nature which
In a minute gave way

One axon escapes along the current leaves to try the woods and become less sensitive. Others are inflammatory, and strike into the cell wall running fast and even quickly for dendritic impact. This is the end of neural space. Collect any words left and combine into a final signal; the terminal branch will establish a new connection with a light touch and no actual damage.

I can't think about you without
thinking about music
so remove from me forever now
and meadows hills and woods give it up

Cataracts come to me
from the glacier of sleep;
Wind-up creatures hear the call,
children reform on each page
fresh flowers,
and a baby stamps on their mother's arm –
On the way to a tree
the joys of the earth fade, their glory disappears;
the morning of the sky flees
and the futile shadows of the earth rise
with the clouds and the sun - *stay with me, guys* –

Everything they've left I carry with me
overhead an unemphatic sunspot
streaming light through the morning's red fingers
turns into drops of sweat
trickling through a finished haircut
tolerant as a parallel text
I cannot get up
beloved
as the sugar drops
through the fog nailed
to the door
completing its swing
from the ceiling plaster falls
like the three halves of a muffin
pale morning sunshine milk and butter
Death is a milkman from Hyndland

The sun riots and the trees turn to water
making the tear gas worse
The road splits in the yellow forest
where I bent in the bushes
and was taken
Thunderstorms occur

but I am calm
The tears have been licked from my eyes
Tell my friends and any children you care about
Not to cry for me, I am leaving now
Push me to the heart of your outermost hole
And we'll all go separately
Picking wild thyme on the mountain
Very happy to be done

The baby spirit says, *Hit him with your hammer.*
The finite hammer under my pillow dissolves.

The ghost baby says, *Take off your scarf:*

Two covers one, here
Is three, here two goes under three

Cross the fabric of
The scarf at one point,

A clockwise turn,
The knot for nothing unfolds

Here three, here two,
Here one,

He can free himself

He told himself

You told yourself

It's time to stop thinking

About the dog

Acknowledgements

The section beginning "Poppers and grass…" revises a small amount of material in sections 1 and 10 of Andrew Crozier's "Free Running Bitch" (An *Andrew Crozier Reader*, edited by Ian Brinton, Carcanet, 2012, pp.237-244).

The section beginning "The you you destroyed…" incorporates, translates and revises a few lines from the opening to Rainer Maria Rilke's "Requiem Für Wolf Graf Von Kalckreuth" (*Gedichte 1895 bis 1910*, Insel Verlag, 1996, pp.422-426; 422).

Acknowledgements

LAY OUT YOUR UNREST

www.ingramcontent.com/pod-product-compliance
Lightning Source LLC
Chambersburg PA
CBHW071943020426
42331CB00010B/2990